What on Earth?
Life in the Tundra

Brrrrr, it's cold!

Crack!

What is this walrus doing?

Turn this page for the answer.

Published in 2005 in the United States by Children's Press,
an imprint of Scholastic Library Publishing,
90 Sherman Turnpike, Danbury, CT 06816

ISBN 0-516-25316-6 (Lib. Bdg.)

A CIP catalog record for this title is available from the Library of Congress.

Printed and bound in China.

Editor: Ronald Coleman
Senior Art Editor: Carolyn Franklin
DTP Designer: Mark Williams

Picture Credits Julian Baker: 8, 9, 11, Elizabeth Branch: 1,
2, 24, John Francis: 6, 7, B and C Alexander, NHPA: 22, 23,
27, T. Kitchin and V Hurst, NHPA: 26, Genny Anderson: 17,
NASA: 26(r), Corel: 3, 8, 9, 10, 11, 13, 14, 15, 16, 18, 20,
21, 30, 31, John Foxx: 19, Corbis: 25, PhotoDisc: 28, 29

Cover © 2005 Theo Allofs/Corbis Images

What on Earth?

Making an airhole!

A walrus uses its tusks to
make a hole up through the
ice to breathe. Its tusks can
grow up to three feet (one
meter) long.

What on Earth? Life in the Tundra

PENNY CLARKE

A fox changes color?

Why?

Turn to page 20 and find out!

children's press®

A Division of Scholastic Inc.

NEW YORK • TORONTO • LONDON • AUCKLAND • SYDNEY

MEXICO CITY • NEW DELHI • HONG KONG

DANBURY, CONNECTICUT

Contents

What on Earth?

Non-stop flight!

Bar-tailed godwits are birds that make the longest non-stop migration. They fly over 6,000 miles (9,656 kilometers) from Alaska to Australia in only five or six days.

Introduction

The tundra is land around the North Pole. It is one of the coldest and bleakest places on Earth. The winters are very dark and very cold. The summers are short and only slightly less cold. Life is hard for the plants, animals, and people who make it their home. They have had to adapt to cope with the extreme cold and the biting winds which whip across the tundra all year long.

Where does the word "tundra" come from?

The word "tundra" comes from Finland and means a "treeless plain". No trees grow on the tundra, because the soil is frozen!

How cold is it?

The average temperature is -18°F (-28°C) which is cold, but not the coldest place on Earth. The coldest temperature ever recorded was -129°F (-89°C) in Antarctica near the South Pole.

What Is the Tundra?

The word "tundra" describes the cold, treeless land which lies around the North Pole. The tundra has long, cold winters. A blanket of snow covers everything in winter, and the ground is **frozen hard** all year long. Even in summer, frost is common.

In the winter it is dark for weeks at a time. Summers last a few months, but the sun never sets. That's why the tundra is called "the land of the midnight sun".

Willow grouse

Caribou

Red-backed vole

6

White-tailed sea eagle

In the tundra, wolves work as a team to separate a musk ox calf from the herd.

Herd of musk oxen

Wolves

Musk ox calf

Lichen

Where Is the Tundra?

Tundra regions are only found in the northern hemisphere, close to the Arctic Circle. The most northern points of North America, Europe and Asia all have areas of tundra. In the southern hemisphere, no land lies close to the frozen continent of Antarctica, so tundra conditions **do not** exist there.

Northern Hemisphere

Arctic Circle

North America

Atlantic Ocean

Equator

Pacific Ocean

South America

Antarctica

Southern Hemisphere

Areas of tundra around the world are shown on these two maps (*above*).

Does the climate of the tundra vary?

The climate of the tundra varies little across North America, northern Europe and Asia, so the plants and animals are similar. Wolves and Arctic foxes travel far north over the tundra in summer.

Polar bears like the cold...

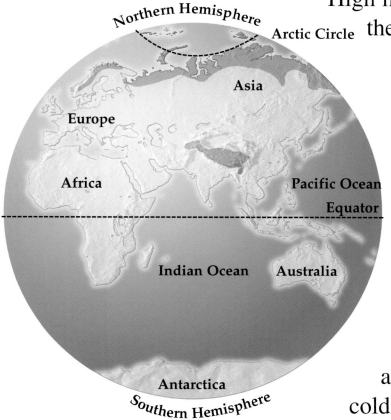

High mountains like the Andes, the Alps and the Himalayas have areas where the temperature and plant life are like the Arctic tundra. Scientists call these areas "alpine tundra" to show they are **different**. The main difference is the length of the seasons. Regions of alpine tundra are very cold, but their winters are shorter and summers are longer than those of the Arctic tundra.

What happens when winter comes?

...so they go north in winter!

As winter comes, the wolves and foxes move south to follow their prey. They continue to hunt birds like the willow grouse, and animals like caribou. Many of the birds in the tundra fly to a warmer place in winter. This journey to another climate is called migration.

Why Is It So Cold?

When the sun shines directly overhead it is at its hottest. But the sun is never directly over the tundra so it never gets hot there, even in summer.

How tall is a musk oxen?

Male musk oxen can be 5 feet (1.5 meters) tall at shoulder height. Musk oxen are one of the few large mammals that can survive on the tundra.

why does it stay cool?

Summer

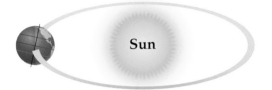

N

United States

Equator

S

The tundra stays cool because the sun hardly reaches it. When it does the sun's rays have cooled so much that the tundra never really warms up. It is so cool that most summer days are less than 50°F (10°C).

Winter

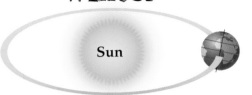

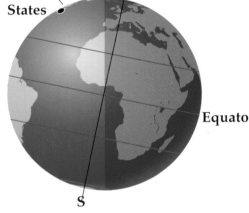

N

United States

Equator

S

The sun is hottest near the Equator. As you can see, the North and South Poles are a long way from the Equator which makes them the coldest places on Earth!

What on Earth?

Is it a hump?

No, the hair on the musk oxen's shoulders is so thick it looks like a hump!

11

What Is the Aurora Borealis?

In winter, spectacular colored lights sometimes fill the sky over the tundra. Called the "Aurora Borealis" or "Northern Lights", this fantastic natural display may only last for a few minutes, and then it vanishes. In past times the lights gave rise to myths about gods and monsters — "Aurora" was the Ancient Romans' goddess of dawn and "Borealis" the Ancient Greeks' god of the north wind.

What causes them?

Gigantic explosions (flares) on the sun's surface thrust tiny particles out into space at speeds of about 100 miles (161 kilometers) a second. They reach Earth around 24 hours later. As they travel down into Earth's atmosphere, they collide with particles in the air. It is these collisions that cause this special light.

What colors are they?

These collisions take place at different heights in Earth's atmosphere. The height of each collision creates a different color. The Aurora Borealis makes purple, blue, green and bright red lights that flicker across the dark sky. It looks like fireworks exploding in the sky.

How powerful are they?

The lights have more electrical power than anything else in the world. They can cause power outages and problems with satellites up in space.

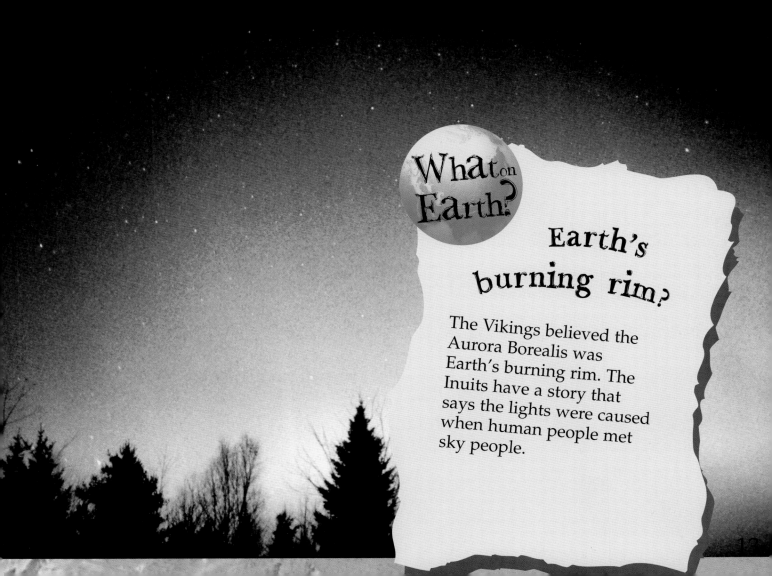

What on Earth?

Earth's burning rim?

The Vikings believed the Aurora Borealis was Earth's burning rim. The Inuits have a story that says the lights were caused when human people met sky people.

Can Anything Live on the Tundra?

Many plants and animals live on the tundra. But they have had to adapt to living with long winters, little daylight, and very cold temperatures. Even in the short summers only the surface thaws. The soil below stays frozen. As a result, the melted snow cannot drain away. This makes the ground very soggy and an excellent breeding ground for insects. Blackflies and mosquitoes appear in an explosion of huge clouds each summer.

What's special about caribous' hooves?

Caribou have big hooves that spread out, giving the animal a better grip as it moves across the snow. The caribou also use their hooves to dig down to find plants buried in the snow.

It must be winter!

In winter the Arctic fox grows a very thick white coat. This disguises it and also protects it from the cold. As a result it can curl up on the snow and sleep, even in temperatures well below freezing.

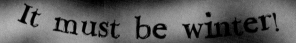

What on Earth?

Too cold for cold-blooded animals?

The tundra is too cold for cold-blooded animals like snakes and frogs. They need warmth to be able to move, breathe or feed. Insects like flies and mosquitoes are cold-blooded and they live on the tundra, but only during the summer.

How Do Plants Survive?

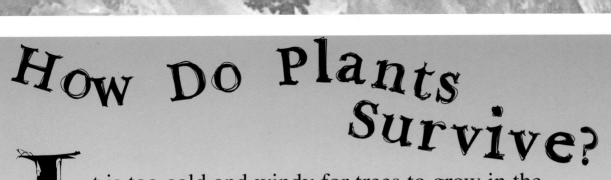

It is too cold and windy for trees to grow in the tundra. Most plants there grow close to the ground. Lichens, mosses, and small cushion-shaped flowers are most common. A **cushion-shape** helps the plant warm quickly when the sun returns.

What on Earth?

small but very old!

Lichens grow very slowly and some types can live for up to 4,000 years! Lichens (*opposite*) are very small and only grow where there is very little pollution. They have spores, like a fern plant, instead of seeds.

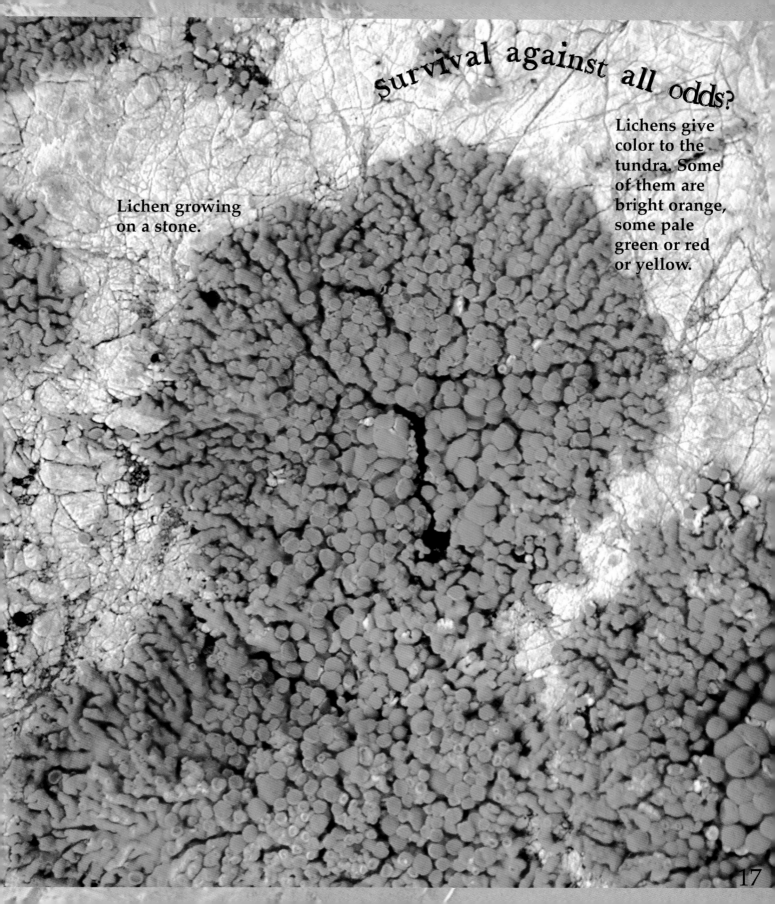

Survival against all odds?

Lichen growing on a stone.

Lichens give color to the tundra. Some of them are bright orange, some pale green or red or yellow.

Can Birds Survive There?

In the summer, birds migrate to the tundra where they nest and breed. The rich supply of insects they feed on will die out as winter approaches. The birds migrate again before snow and ice return to cover the tundra. Many birds fly south to winter in warmer places, often traveling **huge** distances.

Do all birds migrate?

Most birds migrate to avoid winter on the tundra. But the willow grouse and the eagle only migrate as far as the taiga forests, south of the tundra.

Eagle

Willow grouse

What is the taiga?

Taiga is a Russian word which means "land of little sticks". It is a huge belt of thin conifer forests south of the tundra.

Nighttime hunter?

Snowy owls (*left*) hunt in the daytime as well as the night. This is very rare for owls. In summer snowy owls hunt small animals over the tundra. In the winter they hunt ducks and small rodents in the forest.

What on Earth?

Silent and deadly?

Most bird feathers make some noise as they fly through the air. The fluffy edges of an owl's feathers soften any noise so it can **swoop** unheard on its prey.

Whooshsssss!

19

What About Mammals?

Mammals are warm-blooded animals. This means they do not rely on the temperature of the air for warmth. Twenty-three species of **mammals,** including wolves, foxes, caribou, hares, and lemmings can be found on the tundra. Polar bears have adapted so well to the cold that in winter they go far out onto the **frozen** Arctic Ocean to catch seals through the ice.

Arctic hare

A change of coat?

The Arctic hare's coat turns white in winter. This helps it to hide from foxes.

Arctic fox

Two coats?

When the Arctic fox prowls the tundra in summer, its coat is brown. This helps it blend in better to hunt its prey. As winter approaches its coat begins to change. By the time the tundra is snow-covered the fox's coat is very thick and white. It will stay like this until spring.

What on Earth?

Yum yum!

Voles and lemmings usually have lots of babies but when food is scarce they have fewer young. So Arctic foxes and snowy owls, who feed on them, go hungry.

Follow the herd?

In summer, wolves hunt herds of caribou and musk oxen that graze on the tundra. As winter approaches and the herds retreat to the forests, the wolves follow, too.

Do People Live in the Tundra?

Yes, despite the bitter cold, people do live in the tundra. The first people there probably followed herds of caribou as they moved onto the tundra to graze during the summer. Life is **hard**, but there is plenty of food in summer: fish, meat and birds' eggs. Meat and fish can also be preserved for the winter. Animal furs provide warm clothing.

Wolf to dog?

According to legend the first sled dogs were bred from captured wolves. Throughout the tundra the people living there have their own dog breeds: huskies in Siberia, malamutes in Alaska and the Canadian Eskimo dog in Canada.

Dog to snowmobile!

Sleds pulled by teams of dogs used to be the best way to travel across the frozen tundra. Each dog had its place in the team, with the strongest as the leader.

Today snowmobiles have replaced dog sleds as a faster way to cross frozen, snow-covered ground.

Where do the Sami live?

The Sami are people who graze their reindeer on the tundra. The Sami have lived in Lapland in northern Scandinavia for thousands of years.

What on Earth?

Eat your greens!

Apart from plant shoots in spring and berries in autumn, the people of the tundra eat little fruit or vegetables — but are still healthy!

Does the Tundra Change?

Earth has existed for billions of years. During this time its climate has changed — and continues to change. At times Earth has been much warmer, or colder, than it is now. In very cold periods, called **ice ages**, ice covered northern Europe and North America. Beyond these huge areas of ice, the tundra stretched much further south than it does **today**.

When was the last ice age?

The last ice age ended about 10,000 years ago. At its peak, ice sheets over a mile thick covered half of North America. Brrr!

Where did woolly mammoths live?

Fossils (the remains of ancient living things) can show how the climate has changed. Fossils of woolly mammoths, deer, bears, and other tundra animals have been found as far south as Missouri, USA; London, England, and Paris, France.

What on Earth?

Hairy raincoat!

The polar bear, the largest of all bears, is well equipped for the Arctic. Its thick fur coat keeps it warm and is water-repellent, too!

What Is the Tundra Like Now?

Changes to Earth's climate are felt everywhere. Global warming is partly due to pollution and the burning of fossil fuels far to the south of the tundra. This makes the tundra winters shorter and less cold than they used to be. Since tundra summers are becoming longer, more of the permafrost (ground that never thaws) is now thawing.

What effect are humans having?

The huge open spaces of the tundra where few people live seemed ideal for building oil pipelines. But as more of the permafrost thaws, the ground supporting the pipelines becomes unstable. It shifts and sinks unevenly which might crack the pipes. Then floods of oil would spill out.

What on Earth?

What is global warming?

Methane and carbon dioxide gases are believed to be a major cause of global warming. The tundra contains more methane than anywhere else. As the tundra thaws, methane and carbon dioxide gases are released into the atmosphere.

Satellite photograph of Earth and its ozone layer.

How would you survive in the tundra?

Although the tundra is home to polar bears and wolves, you are more likely to die of the cold than to be eaten by an animal. Be prepared if you travel across the tundra because if you get lost and can't catch any food there isn't much to eat apart from a tasty diet of **reindeer moss!**

Tundra dangers

Polar bears prefer to eat seals and only attack humans if they are provoked. If a bear approaches — don't run. The bear can run faster than you.

Wolves are usually afraid of humans but will attack if they have a disease called rabies. Make a loud noise to frighten the wolves away.

Hypothermia is when you get so cold that your body temperature drops dangerously low. Try to get out of the cold and light a fire, but do not warm up again too quickly as you could go into shock!

What to take checklist

Be sure to wear **mittens, hats and thick socks** to stop you from getting frostbite. Make sure you take **snow shoes** so you don't fall through the ice. Don't get lost — be sure to take a **compass**. Take a good pair of warm **boots** and a **box of matches** to light a fire at night. Take an **alarm** to scare off attacking wolves and be certain to take a **two-way radio** to call for help. Learn to build an igloo or remember to take a strong **tent** and a **sleeping bag** or you will freeze. Take freeze-dried food with you as it doesn't go bad.

Don't fall in the water!

The narwhal is a strange looking whale. It has a large tooth growing through its upper lip to form a tusk (*right*). In the Middle Ages its tusk was thought to be a unicorn's horn.

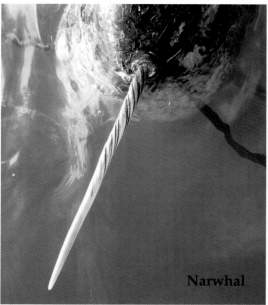

Narwhal

Tundra Facts

Even though the fur is white, the skin of a polar bear is actually black like its nose!

A type of tundra grass called cotton grass looks like cotton balls on sticks.

Arctic terns migrate 22,000 miles (35,405 kilometers) between the North and South poles. After seven years of migrating, they will have flown as far as the distance between Earth and the Moon.

Polar bears don't drink water. They get all the liquid they need from the fishes, seals and other food they eat.

The horned puffin is such a bad flyer that it must run on the surface of the water before it takes off.

Polar bear watching is now an important tourist attraction in northern Canada.

Moose

28

Glossary

caribou North American name for the European reindeer

cold-blooded term describing animals whose body temperature varies according to the temperature of the air around them

Equator imaginary line around the middle of Earth

fossil fuels natural fuels, like coal, gas, and oil, formed from the remains of long-dead living things. For example, coal is mostly made up of the remains of ancient plants

mammal animal with fur or hair which is fed on its mother's milk while it is a baby

methane colorless, odorless gas which doesn't smell and burns easily

migrate/migration long journey made by some birds and animals, usually twice a year, to find food

northern hemisphere the part of the world that is north of the Equator

particles tiny pieces of matter

permafrost ground that is always frozen

southern hemisphere the part of the world that is south of the Equator

species group of plants or animals that look and behave the same

woolly mammoths creatures that lived about 10,000 years ago

Puffin

What Do You Know About the Tundra?

1. What does the word "tundra" mean in the Finnish language?

2. What is special about caribou hooves?

3. Why are plants very small in the tundra?

4. Why do insects breed so well after the snow melts?

5. Why is the tundra never warm?

6. Does the willow grouse migrate?

7. Have polar bears adapted to the cold?

8. What replaced sleds and dog teams in the tundra?

9. What are methane and carbon dioxide gases thought to cause?

10. Where do bar-tailed godwits migrate to in winter?

Can you guess how much a grizzly bear weighs?

Go to page 32 for the answers.

Grizzly bears are ranging further north as the climate becomes warmer.

Index

Pictures are shown in **bold** type.

Answers

1. Treeless (See page 5)
2. Caribou hooves spread out to grip the snow better (See page 14)
3. This helps them shelter from the icy winds (See page 16)
4. The melted snow makes the ground soggy (See page 14)
5. The sun hardly reaches the tundra (See page 11)
6. Only as far south as the taiga forests (See page 18)
7. Yes, polar bears go further north in the winter (See page 20)
8. Snowmobiles (See page 22)
9. Global warming (See page 26)
10. Australia (See contents page)

An adult grizzly bear weighs up to 1,150 pounds (522 kg). That's the weight of nine and a half washing machines!